Illuminated
Life

I LLUMINATED
LIFE *Monastic
Wisdom for
Seekers of
Light*

JOAN CHITTISTER

ORBIS BOOKS

Maryknoll, New York 10545

Second Printing, September 2010

The Catholic Foreign Mission Society of America (Maryknoll) recruits and trains people for overseas missionary service. Through Orbis Books, Maryknoll aims to foster the international dialogue that is essential to mission. The books published, however, reflect the opinions of their authors and are not meant to represent the official position of the society. To obtain more information about Maryknoll or Orbis Books, please visit our website at www.maryknollsociety.org.

Published in 2000 by Orbis Books, P.O. Box 302,
Maryknoll, NY 10545-0302 U.S.A.

Manufactured in the United States of America

Library of Congress Cataloging-in-Publication Data

Chittister, Joan.
    Illuminated life : monastic wisdom for seekers of light / Joan Chittister.
      p. cm.
    Includes bibliographical references.
    ISBN 978-1-57075-878-2 (pbk.)
    1. Christian life – Catholic authors. 2. Spiritual life – Catholic Church. 3. Monastic and religious life. I. Title.

BX2350.2 .C526 2000
248.8'94 – dc21   99-058636

*This book is dedicated
to all the busy contemplatives around me
who have challenged my vision
and deepened my soul
just by bringing the presence of God
wherever they happened to be at the time
and, in particular, to Mary Margaret Kraus, OSB,
past prioress, Benedictine Sisters of Erie,
who exudes what this book is about.*

Contents

Acknowledgments 11

Illuminated Life:
Being Contemplative in the Midst of Chaos 13

Awareness 21

Beauty 25

Community 30

Dailiness 35

Enlightenment 40

Faith 44

Growth   49

Humility   54

Interiority   59

Justice   64

Kindness   70

Lectio, the Art of Holy Reading   74

Metanoia, Call to Conversion   78

Nature   83

Openness   87

Prayer   91

Quest   95

Re-creation 100

Silence 105

Time 109

Understanding 113

Vision 117

Work 121

Xenophilia, the Love of Strangers 126

Yearning 131

Zeal 135

Across the Centuries 139

Bibliography 143

Acknowledgments

People illumine our lives as little else has the capacity to do. I know because this book, as well as most of the rest of my life, is lived in the light of good friends and competent council. Many have contributed to this endeavor, made it stronger, given it more depth, more precision.

I am particularly grateful to Mary Lou Kownacki, OSB, who prompted this work, as she has so many others of my projects. I am never unaware of the insights and responses of Marlene Bertke, OSB, Jean Lavin, OSB, Rita Panciera, RSM, Anne McCarthy, OSB, Brother Thomas Bezanson, Christine Vladimiroff, OSB, and Linda Romey, OSB, who gave it considerable and contemplative attention.

I am most grateful to Andrea Lee, IHM, President, College of

St. Catherine, St. Paul, Minn., for the gracious, comfortable, and recklessly generous contribution of campus facilities and support services that made this writing possible. With the help of the college staff, the community of the Sisters of St. Joseph there, and the personal support of Mary Delaney and the entire Delaney family this work time itself was a rich and contemplative experience.

I am always grateful and ever in awe of the investment of time, competence, and professionalism of Mary Lee Farrell, GNSH, and Mary Grace Hanes, OSB, as they negotiate the mysteries of the publishing world and bring these books to light.

Finally, I know that without the office management and general facilitation of Maureen Tobin, OSB, during these long periods, there would be no publications — and even less reflection time — in my life.

To all these people I present the beginning of ideas worth pursuing more thoroughly, more deeply, always.

Illuminated Life
Being Contemplative in the Midst of Chaos

THIS BOOK TALKS ABOUT YOUR LIFE — the one you fear is not spiritual because of its complexities and concerns. Spirituality, you are certain, is the province of those who manage to escape from the pressures of life. But if withdrawal is of the essence of the spiritual life, then whole generations of spiritual sages have been wrong. This book is about qualities the world's most ancient of seekers say are the cardinal components of a contemplative life. And "escape," you will notice, is not one of the elements of this long-standing spiritual alphabet. The truly spiritual person, tradition teaches us, knows that spirituality is conccrned with how to live a full life, not an empty one. Real spirituality is life illumined by a compelling search for wholeness. It is contemplation at the eye of chaos. It is life lived to the full.

All we have in life is life. Things — the cars, the houses, the educations, the jobs, the money — come and go, turn to dust between our fingers, change and disappear. Things do not make life, life. The gift of life, the secret of life, is that it must be developed from the inside out, from what we bring to it from within ourselves, not from what we collect or consume as we go through it, not even from what we experience in the course of it. It is not circumstance that makes or destroys a life. Anyone who has survived the death of a lover, the loss of a position, the end of a dream, the enmity of a friend knows that.

It is the way we live each of the circumstances of life, the humdrum as well as the extraordinary, the daily as well as the defining moments, that determines the quality of our lives. Rich people are often deeply unhappy. Poor people are often blissfully contented. Old people know things about life that young people have yet to learn. Women have a different perspective on life than men do. Young people have hopes that old people cannot claim. Men have a sense of living that women are only now beginning to learn. Yet, all of them, each of them — each of us — has the latitude to live life either well or poorly. Ironically enough, it is a matter of decision. And the decision is ours.

Centuries ago, some men and women intent on living life beyond the obvious developed a life style, a set of values, an attitude of mind, a way of going through life designed to bring life to life. These monastic wisdom figures reaffirmed for every generation the balance which becoming whole requires This book is about those values. Those attitudes, those insights, have been tried over time and found to be true. Most of all, they can be developed by anyone in any situation. They tell us how to keep things in perspective, how to live life well, how to see the life beyond life. Those qualities are available to us yet. They make us contemplatives in the midst of chaos.

Time presses upon us and tells us we're too busy to be contemplative, but our souls know better. Souls die from lack of reflection. Responsibilities dog us and tell us we're too involved with the "real" world to be concerned about the spiritual question. But it is always spiritual questions that make the difference in the way we go about our public responsibilities. Marriage, business, children, professions are all defined to keep contemplation out. We go about them as if there were no inherent spiritual dimension to each of them when the fact of the matter is that no one needs contemplation more than the harried mother, the irritable father, the ambitious executive, the striving professional, the poor woman, the sick man. Then, in those situations, we need reflection, understanding, meaning, peace of soul more than ever. People from all states of life, in all periods of time have known the need, have pursued the presence of God in the most ungodly of times and situations. This book recalls those qualities and applies them to the present.

Religion is about ritual, about morals, about systems of thought, all of them good but all of them incomplete. Spirituality is about coming to consciousness of the sacred. It is in that consciousness that perspective comes, that peace comes. It is in that consciousness that a person comes to wholeness.

Life is not an exercise to be endured. It is a mystery to be unfolded.

Life comes from the living of it. The attitudes we bring to it and the understandings we take away from each of the moments that touch us constitute the depth of soul we bring to all the most mundane events of life. They measure the quality of our lives. The truth is that life is the only commodity each of us actually owns. It is the only thing in the universe over which we have any real control whatsoever, slim as that may be.

It is a busy world. A frightfully busy world sometimes. We live in a world the speed and pressures of which consume us, drain our souls, dry out our hearts, damp our spirits and make living more a series of duties than a kind of joyful mystery. We spend time making telephone callbacks, doing the shopping, hauling the laundry, running errands through narrow, crowded streets, grinding through routines, going to meetings, answering question after question, doing repetitive motions, standing in lines of one kind or another, making the long commute, falling into bed late — too late — day after day, night after night. We close our eyes at the end of the day and wonder where life has gone.

We spend life too tired to garden, too distracted to read, too busy to talk, too plagued by people and deadlines to organize our lives, to reflect on our futures, to appreciate our present. We simply go on, day after day. Where is what it means to be human in all of that? Where is God in all of that? How shall we ever get the most out of life if life itself is our greatest obstacle to it? What does it mean to be spiritual, to be contemplative, in the midst of the private chaos that clutters our paltry little lives? Where can we go for a model of another way to live when we have no choice but to live the way we do?

The desert monastics, alone in the wilderness of fourth-century Egypt, wrestled with the elements of life, plumbed its basics, tested its truths, and passed on their wisdom to those who sought it out. Thousands of people saw the difference in their stripped-down, simple lives and trekked out to their small monasteries to ask what it was that could wring such meaning out of such apparent deprivation. The abbas and ammas, the spiritual fathers and mothers of the desert, left words for the ages to live by. Fifteen centuries later, their words still ring through time, calling each of us to take as rudders and as beacons a series of values meant to bring depth, meaning, and happiness to the most cluttered, most pressured, most parched of us.

Illuminated Life is a summons. It invites us to quit looking for spiritual techniques and psychological quick-fixes to give substance to our lives. It asks us to remember again the spiritual direction that has stood the test of time. It asks us to go inside ourselves to clear out the debris of the heart rather than to concentrate on trying to control the environment and situations around us. It leads us to see into the present with the eye of the soul so that we can see into the glimpse of heaven that each life carries within itself. It takes us inside ourselves and leads us back out of ourselves at the same time.

Abba Sisoes said: "Seek God, and not where God lives." We live and breathe, grow and develop in the womb of God. And yet we seek God elsewhere — in defined places, in special ways, on mountaintops and in caves, on specific days and with special ceremonies. But the life that is full of light knows that God is not over there, God is here. And for the taking. The only question is how.

waReNess

A brother went to see Abba Moses in his hermitage at Scetis and begged him for a word. And the old man said: "Go and sit in your cell, and your cell will teach you everything."

WHAT IS RIGHT IN FRONT OF US we see least. We take the plants in the room for granted. We pay no attention to the coming of night. We miss the look of invitation on a neighbor's face. We see only ourselves in action and miss the cocoon around us. As a result, we run the risk of coming out of every situation with no more than when we went into it.

Learning to notice the obvious, the colors that touch our psyches, the shapes that vie for our attention, the looks on the faces of those who stand before us blurred by familiarity, blank with anonymity — the context in which we find our distracted selves — is the beginning of contemplation. Awareness of the power of the present — monastic mindfulness — is the essence of the contemplative life and common to all contemplative traditions. "Oh, wonder of wonders," the Sufi master says, "I chop wood. I draw water from the well." I live in the present, in other words. I know that what is, is the presence of God for me. "The first step of humility is to 'keep the reverence of God always before our eyes' and never forget it," the Rule of Benedict says. See everything in life as sacred. This neighborhood calls something out in us. This tree stirs feeling in us. This work touches hope in us. Everything in life, in fact, is speaking to us of something. It is only when we learn to ask what the world around us is saying to us at this very moment, in this particular situation, that we tend to the seedbed of the soul.

Awareness puts us into contact with the universe. It mines every relationship, unmasks every event, every moment, for the meaning that is under the meaning of it. The question is not so much what is going on in the room, but what is happening to me because of it? What do I see here of God that I could not see otherwise? What is God demanding of my heart as a result of each event, each situation, each person in my life? Etty Hillesum, Jewish prisoner in one of Hitler's concentration camps, saw the goodness in her German guards. That is contemplation, that is the willingness to see as God sees. It does not change the difficulty, the boredom, the evil of a pernicious, an insidious situation, perhaps, but it can change the texture of our own hearts, the quality of our own responses, the depth of our own understandings. Without awareness, enemies stay forever only enemies and life is forever bland.

Until I become truly aware of the world in which I live, I cannot possibly get more out of a situation than a mere outline of reality, a kind of caricature of time. It takes a lifetime to really understand that God is in what is standing in front of me. Most of life is spent looking, straining to see the God in the mist, behind the cloud, beyond the dark. It is when we face God in one another, in creation, in the moment, that the real spiritual journey begins.

Everything in life is meant to stretch me beyond my superficial self to my better self, to the Ultimate Good who is God. But before that can happen, I must be alive in it myself. I must ask of everything in life: What is this saying to me about life? Why? Because when we cease to look deeply at all the parts of our lives, our souls are already dead.

To be a contemplative I must ask always, of everything: What is there in this of God for me?

**eauty**

One night bandits came to the hermitage of an old monastic and said: "We have come to take away everything in your cell." And the monastic said, "Take whatever you see, my sons." The bandits gathered up everything they found and went away. But they left behind a little bag with silver candlesticks. When the monastic saw it, he picked it up and ran after them, shouting. "Take these, take these. You forgot them and they are the most beautiful of all."

W HAT MAY BE MOST MISSING in this highly technological world of ours is beauty. We value efficiency instead. We want functionalism over art. We create trash. We bask in kitsch. But beauty, right proportion in all things, harmony in the universe of our lives, truth in appearances, eludes us. We paint over good wood. We prefer plastic flowers to wild flowers. We reproduce the Pietà in plastics. We forego the natural and the real for the gaudy and the pretentious. We are, as a people, awash in the banal. A loss of commitment to beauty may be the clearest sign we have that we have lost our way to God. Without beauty we miss the glory of the face of God in the here and now.

Beauty is the most provocative promise we have of the Beautiful. It lures us and calls us and leads us on. Souls thirst for beauty and thrive on it and by it nourish hope. It is Beauty that magnetizes the contemplative, and it is the duty of the contemplative to give beauty away so that the rest of the world may, in the midst of squalor, ugliness, and pain, remember that beauty is possible.

Beauty feeds contemplation, and Beauty is its end. A sense of Beauty evokes in us consciousness of the eternal in the temporal. It calls us beyond both the present and the past to that everlasting Now where Beauty dwells in perpetuity.

Beauty, in other words, lifts life out of the anesthetizing clichés of the pedestrian. An encounter with the beautiful lifts our eyes beyond the commonplace and gives us a reason for going on, for ranging beyond the mundane, for endeavoring ourselves always to become more than we are. In the midst of struggle, in the depths of darkness, in the throes of ugliness, beauty brings with it a realization that the best in life is, whatever the cost, really possible.

Beauty takes us beyond the visible to the height of consciousness, past the ordinary to the mystical, away from the expedient to the endlessly true. Beauty sustains the human heart in the midst of pain and despair. Whatever the dullness of a world stupefied by the mediocre, in the end beauty is able, by penetrating our own souls, to penetrate the ugliness of a world awash in the cheap, the tawdry, the imitative, the excessive, and the cruel. To have seen a bit of the Beauty out of which beauty comes is a deeply spiritual experience. It shouts to us always, "More. There is yet more."

Beauty is not a matter of having enough money to buy anything in sight. It is a matter of having enough taste to recognize quality, depth, truth, harmony when we see it. "Beauty is truth and truth beauty / That's all we know and all we need to know," the poet John Keats wrote. A thing is beautiful, in other words, when it really is what it purports to be. There are cures, of course, for a deprivation of spirit. We could take down the billboards that turn the landscape into a junkyard of old ideas. We could clear away the clash of colors and things that saturate space and make seeing into the soul of a thing impossible. We could refuse to allow people to turn marble statues into plastic replicas. We could study the order, the harmony, the proportion of a flower. We could strain our eyes to look for what is beneath the obvious in the wrinkles of age, the misshapened knuckles of a worker's hands, the meaning in every moment, the ultimate in every possibility, the essence of every encounter. Or we could simply own one soul-shattering piece of art ourselves, put it up in a solitary place over and against the commonplace which normally surrounds us. We could let it seep into the center of the self until we find that we can never be satisfied again, anesthetized again, by the visual platitudes of the world in which we live.

What we do not nourish within ourselves cannot exist in the world around us because we are its microcosm. We cannot moan the loss of quality in our world and not ourselves seed the beautiful in our wake. We cannot decry the loss of the spiritual and continue ourselves to function only on the level of the vulgar. We cannot hope for fullness of life without nurturing fullness of soul. We must seek beauty, study beauty, surround ourselves with beauty. To revivify the soul of the world, we ourselves must become beauty. Where we are must be more beautiful because we have been there than it was before our coming.

To be contemplative we must remove the clutter from our lives, surround ourselves with beauty, and consciously, relentlessly, persistently, give it away until the tiny world for which we ourselves are responsible begins to reflect the raw beauty that is God.

# Community

Cassian taught this: Abba John, abbot of a large monastery, went to Abba Paesius who had been living for forty years far off in the desert. As John was very fond of Paesius and could therefore speak freely with him, he said to him, "What good have you done by living here in retreat for so long, and not being easily disturbed by anyone?" Paesius replied, "Since I have lived in solitude, the sun has never seen me eating." Abba John said back to him, "As for me, since I have been living with others, it has never seen me angry."

S OLITUDE, a sometimes romanticized and often exaggerated element of the contemplative life, has its own struggles, of course. But, the desert monastics imply, when we choose solitude as the kiln for our souls, the temptation can be to gauge spiritual development by a lesser standard than the Gospel describes. When a person lives alone, the ancients knew, it can be very beguiling to confuse practice with holiness. If the measuring stick of spirituality is simply rigid physical asceticism and fidelity to the rules, the fasts, the routines, then spiritual ripening is simply a matter of some kind of spiritual arithmetic. We count up what we've done, what we've "given up," what we've avoided and count ourselves holy. The problem, these great masters of the spiritual life knew, is that such a measure is a partial one. To claim full human development, total spiritual maturity, outside the realm of the human community is to claim the impossible.

The real contemplative does not have to withdraw from life to find

God. The real contemplative hears the voice of God in the voice of the other, sees the face of God in the face of the other, knows the will of God in the person of the other, serves the heart of God by addressing the wounds, answering the call of the other. "The most valiant monastics," the Rule of Benedict insists, "are those who live in community. . . . Let permission to live alone be seldom given." St. Basil, an early leader of Eastern Monasticism, asks pointedly, "Whose feet shall the hermit wash?" The implications are clear. It is human community that tests the spiritual grist of the human being.

Community, Abba John teaches, calls us to the kind of relationships that walk us through minefields of personal selfishness, that confront us with moments of personal responsibility, that raise us to the level of personal heroics, and lead us to the rigor of personal compassion day after day after day. It is when we see in the needs of others what we are meant to give away that we become truly empty of ourselves. It is in the challenges of the times that we come to speak the Spirit. It is when we find ourselves dealing with the downright intransigence of the other that we understand our own sin. It is when we recognize in the world around us the call of God to us that our response to the human race becomes the measuring stick of the quality of our souls.

When anger rages in us unabated and unresolved, we obliterate the other in our hearts. When months go by and we never even speak to our neighbors, never seek them out, never stir ourselves out of our hermitages to admit their existence, we deny creation. When advice is something we resist and questions are something we avoid in life, God has no voice by which to call us.

The contemplative sees the Creator in the gleam of the created. God, we come to realize, is indeed everywhere. The goodness we see in the other gives us a glimpse of the face of God. What we learn from the other we learn about ourselves. The honor with which we regard the other unmasks our own theology of creation. The way we react to the needs of the other tells us something about our own needs. The attention we give to another exposes our real sense of the breadth of the universe and stretches it beyond ourselves. We see in others the kind of commitment it takes to go on believing when our own belief falters. We look to others for the kind of vision that expands our own beyond the daily. We depend on others for the kind of wisdom that exceeds mere answers. We hold on to others to find the kind of love that makes life rich with meaning, certain proof of the everlasting love of a God for whom there is no word.

Clearly, in the serious contemplation of our place in the human community lies the quality of our contemplation. To be a real contemplative we must every day take others into the narrow little confines of our lives — and listen to their call to us to be about something greater than ourselves.

Illuminated Life

ailiness

Abba Poemen said about Abba Pior that every single day he made a fresh beginning.

O NE OF THE MOST DIFFICULT, but most seasoning, elements of life is simply the fine art of getting up every morning, of doing what must be done if for no other reason than that it is our responsibility to do it. To face the elements of the day and keep on going takes a peculiar kind of courage. It is in dailiness that we prove our mettle. And it is not easy.

The easy thing is to run away from life. Anyone can do it, and everyone at one time or another wants to. Living through the sterile and the fruitless cycles of life earns no medals, carries no honor. The temptation is to put down the hard parts, to disappear from the heat of the day, to escape from the dullness of the daily, from its pressures and its dry, barren routines when life looks so much more exciting, so much more rewarding, somewhere else.

Few, in the end, ever go, of course. But simply staying where we are because there is nowhere else to go is not the answer. What makes the difference is to stay where we need to be with a sense that dailiness is the real stuff of contemplation. Then the staying becomes more than bearable; it becomes possible.

Regularity has been a mark of the spiritual life in every century, in every tradition. The Rule of Benedict is built on an ordo of prayer, work, and reading that forms the backbone of every day of the monastic life. Why? Because the spiritual life is meant to be dull? No, because the spiritual life is meant to be constant, meant to be centered. The dailiness of spiritual practices, the practices of daily life, focus the heart and concentrate the mind. Incessant agitation, unending variety, constant novelty, a torrent of gadgetry, a life filled with the strange and the unfamiliar irritate the soul and fragment the inner vision.

Dailiness, routine, sameness frees the heart to traffic in more important matters. The desert monastics wove baskets every day of their lives to earn alms for the poor — and, when the baskets went unsold, unbraided them and began again. The purpose was to occupy the body and free the mind. Mindless work — mowing the lawn, sweeping the sidewalk, washing the windows — is not a burden when the mind is full and the heart like a laser beam finds its way to God. We wait for retreats, services, grand gatherings to take us to God, and God is with us all the while. We are just too preoccupied, too disassociated to notice. We run from place to place and thing to thing, we skirt from idea to idea and do not recognize God in the humdrum of the day to day. We give our souls no rest and find them dying from spiritual starvation when we need them most.

Dailiness frees us for the things of God. The important thing is to prepare the mind by prayer and reading, to make the routine parts of life periods of reflection, so that God can be present in mechanical moments in conscious ways. Every day the contemplative makes a new beginning, tries again to plumb the meaning of life, disappears again into the heart of God so present in the world around us if we only realize it. To be a contemplative there must be time for God. The routine parts of life, the dull parts of every day — the commute, the cleaning, the cooking, the waiting times — are gifts of space. Then, while the world goes on around us, the thoughts of God take hold within us. Then we are ready for the chaos that comes with variety, with gadgets, with change, with the whirl of a world in motion.

To be a contemplative we must remember to begin again, day after day, to turn dailiness into time with God.

nlightenment

Amma Syncletica said: "In the beginning, there is struggle and a lot of work for those who come near to God. But after that, there is indescribable joy. It is just like building a fire: at first it's smoky and your eyes water, but later you get the desired result. Thus we ought to light the divine fire in ourselves with tears and effort."

*T*HE IMPORTANT THING TO REMEMBER in the spiritual life is that religion is a means, not an end. When we stop at the level of the rules and the laws, the doctrines and the dogmas — good guides as these may be — and call those things the spiritual life, we have stopped far short of the meaning of life, the call of the divine, the fullness of the self.

Enlightenment is the ability to see beyond all the things we make God to find God. We make religion God and so fail to see godliness where religion is not, though goodness is clear and constant in the simplest of people, the remotest of places. We make national honor God and fail to see the presence of God in other nations, particularly non-Christian nations. We make personal security God and fail to see God in the bleak and barren dimensions of life. We make our own human color the color of God and fail to see God in the one who comes in different guise. We give God gender and miss the spirit of God everywhere in everyone. We separate spirit and matter as if they were two different things, though we know now from quantum physics that matter is simply fields of force made dense by the spirit of Energy. We are one with the Universe, in other words. We are not separate from it or different from it. We are not above it. We are in it, all of us and everything, swimming in an energy that is God. To be enlightened is to see behind the forms to the God who holds them in being.

Enlightenment sees, too, beyond the shapes and icons that intend to personalize God to the God that is too personal, too encompassing, to be any one shape or form or name. Enlightenment takes us beyond our parochialisms to the presence of God everywhere, in everyone, in the universe.

To be enlightened is to be in touch with the God within and around us more than it is to be engulfed in any single way, any one manifestation, any specific denominational or nationalistic construct, however good and well-intentioned it may be.

It is a practice in many monasteries to turn and bow to the sister walking in procession with you after bowing to the altar as you enter chapel for prayer. The meaning of such a monastic custom is clear: God is as much in the world around us, as much in one another, as on that altar or in that chapel. God is the stuff of our lives, the breath of our very souls, calling us always to a heightened understanding of Life in all its forms.

To be enlightened is to know that heaven is not "coming." Heaven is here. We have simply not been able to realize that yet because, like King Arthur and his search for the Holy Grail, we look in all the wrong places, worship all the wrong idols, get fixated on all the wrong notions of God. We are always on our way to somewhere else when this place, the place in which I stand, wherever it is, is the place of my procession into God, the site of my union with the Life that gives life.

To be contemplative I must put down my notions of separateness from God and let God speak to me through everything that seeps through the universe into the pores of my minuscule little life. Then I will find myself, as Abbess Syncletica promises, at the flash point of the divine fire.

aith

Abba Doulas, the disciple of Abba Bessarion, said: When we were walking along the sea one day, I was thirsty, so I said to Abba Bessarion, "Abba, I am very thirsty." Then the old man prayed and said to me, "Then drink from the sea." And the water was sweet when I drank it. So I poured it into a flask so that I would not be thirsty later. Seeing this, the old man asked me, "Why are you doing that?" And I answered, "So that I won't be thirsty later on." Then the old man said, "God is here and God is everywhere."

*F*AITH IS THE GATE, the goal, and the bedrock of the contemplative life. Faith is not denominational. It is confidence in a God we cannot see but know without doubt exists — if for no other reason than that we feel the power of life within us and know our smallness at the same time. Immersed in the awareness of God everywhere, overwhelmed by the effort of living in a consciousness punctuated by death, the contemplative has faith in the process of life.

Contemplative faith is not based on magic or belief in a Great Puppeteer. The contemplative knows simply that the God who gave life sustains it, makes it possible, and has provided everything we need to negotiate it with deep meaning and endless consequence. The contemplative knows what it is to live in the womb of God. The contemplative, the Rule of Benedict says, "prays always," is always in touch with God in whose Life we live.

Faith is beyond denominational purity, more than religious devotion, more than saintly rigor. Faith rests in the arms of God, trusts today and accepts tomorrow because faith knows that whatever the day, God is in it. Where there is possibility without certainty, faith assures. Where there is uncertainty without surety, faith sustains. Where there is confidence that life has purpose even when it does not have clarity, faith is its foundation. Faith lives in the mystery that is God and thrives on life.

Faith is not belief in an afterlife based on today's moral litmus test. To the contemplative "bad" and "good" make no matter. Each has the capacity to become the other. Out of bad much good has come. It is often sin that unmasks us to ourselves and opens the way for growth. Mature virtue is tried virtue, not virtue unassailed. Great good, on the other hand, whatever its effects, has so often deteriorated into arrogance, into a righteousness that vitiates its own rightness. But both of them, both bad and good, lived in the light of God, blanch, are reduced to size in the face of the Life that transcends them.

Life is not a game we win, and God is not a trophy we merit. No matter how "good" we are, we are not good enough for God. On the other hand, no matter how "bad" we are, we can never be outside of God. We can only hope in each instance to come to such a consciousness of God that no lesser gods can capture our attention and no trifling, self-centered gods can keep us from the fullness of awareness that is the fullness of Life. It is the project of life, this coming to Wholeness, this experience of Purpose beyond all purposes, this identification with everything that is.

Life, the contemplative knows, is a process. It is not that all the elements of life, mundane as they may be, do not matter. On the contrary, to the contemplative everything matters. Everything speaks of God, and God is both in and beyond everything.

Having the faith to take life one piece at a time — to live it in the knowledge that there is something of God in this for me now, here, at this moment — is of the essence of happiness. It is not that God is a black box full of tests and trials and treats. It is that life is a step on the way to a God who goes the way with us. However far, however perilous.

The thought of life on a small planet whirling in space is a recipe for despair. It is the source of human anxiety, this thought of having been cut adrift alone and without meaning. To the person of faith, it is this very mystery that pushes us to the edge of our souls where life is the beginning, not the end, and presses us down into the center of our souls where God, the energy of space, waits for us smiling.

To the contemplative, faith is not about having lights turn green before we get to the stop light at the corner or even about having cancerous tumors disappear on command. Faith is about knowing that life is the tabernacle of a living God made small by our meager icons of Being. To the contemplative, it is clear that the many forms of life all reveal in some measure the Life that is their Ground. The life to come, the contemplative knows from having lived this one, will be good.

To be a contemplative, we must have the faith that is beyond our need for magic solutions to daily questions. We must allow the soul to soar far freer than simply to the thought of a God who exaggerates the natural order in our behalf. Faith comes only when we are willing to trust the Blackness that is Light, the hard spots of a fragile world, each of which we would rather have had made easy.

rowth

Abba Mios was asked by a soldier whether God would forgive a sinner. After instructing him at some length, the old man asked him: "Tell me, my dear, if your cloak were torn, would you throw it away?" "Oh, no," the soldier said. "I would mend it and wear it again." And the old man said to him: "Well, if you care that much for your cloak, do you think God does not care as much for a creature?"

ENLIGHTENMENT OPENS THE SOUL to an awareness of the God-life everywhere, to the holiness of life, to the connectedness of the universe, to the realization of the Oneness of creation. It is a consciousness that makes morality and maturity possible, but it is neither morality nor maturity. Union with God is not the perfection of the self, nor a badge of excellence. Union with God is a realization of the living presence of God everywhere, in me, around me, above me, below me. "Before me and behind me, to my right and to my left," as the Irish mystics said.

Union with God is not a static thing which, once achieved, marble-izes the soul into one arrested, unending moment of illumination suspended over life. On the contrary. Life is life. It does not freeze at any time, under any conditions. Life goes on, whatever our consciousness of God. And we with it. We go on grappling with life. We go on growing into awareness. We go on struggling to be worthy of the awareness in which we now walk. And we fail often.

Life is simply not about perfection, because perfection is not something that life offers. Our bodies do not develop to some ultimate state and then become fixed into some eternal form. Scientists tell us that all the protein molecules of our bodies change every six months. Every six months we are made new again, not ostensibly different, perhaps, but new. Nor do our souls reach a static state. Every day we make our souls new again. Every day we rethink old decisions and make new ones. We grapple and struggle and distort and repent over and over again. Every day of our lives we grow a little more into God or a little more into self.

Contemplation has something to do with the ways in which we choose to grow. It is possible to give ourselves over totally to the satisfaction of the self. We can crave and hoard and accumulate and demand obeisance from the rest of the world until our lungs ache from screaming inside and our hearts echo our hollowness. We can cling to the worship of the self forever if we choose. We can spend our whole selves on ourselves, picayune as the topic may be. Western culture not only supports a concentration on the self alone; it encourages it. Getting it all and keeping it forever is the banner under which we march in this century. But there is another choice.

We can choose to grow beyond the self that is a shrine to the idols of the day. We can struggle to put down the notions that choke our souls in the name of pseudo-superiority: that women are invisible, that men are superior, that foreigners are grist for our economic mills, that nature is for our satisfaction alone, that we are, as human beings, above the rest of the universe and beyond its restraints and restrictions. We can, on the other hand, make ourselves our own God. But if we do, we lose the very gift that life is meant to give: the gift of growth. The contemplative lives to grow in unity with the universe.

To be a contemplative we must, then, live in sync with the mind of God, in tune with the rest of the human race and in touch with the weaknesses of our own souls, those places where the love of God breaks in to fill up what we ourselves do not have. Growth is not simply about avoiding sin, whatever we know sin to be as we move from stage to stage in life. Sin, in fact, may be the very thing that brings us to enlightenment. When I am most angry, I know best my need for peace. When I am my most arrogant, I realize how puny is my bravado. When I am most unyielding, I know how isolating is my strength. No, growth — real growth — is about discovering that God stands by, waiting to consume us. If and when we ourselves can ever cease to consume every moment, every person, every event, every experience for ourselves, God can prevail in us.

To be a contemplative it is necessary to set out every morning to grow into more than I was when I began the day by growing into the consciousness of the silent God so great within me.

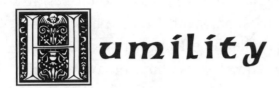# Humility

Abba Xanthias said: "A dog is better than I am because a dog also has love but, unlike I myself, the dog does not pass judgment."

Abba Sarmatas said: "I prefer a person who has sinned if he knows that he sinned and has repented, over a person who has not sinned and considers himself to be righteous."

*H*UMILITY AND CONTEMPLATION are the invisible twins of the spiritual life. One without the other is impossible. In the first place, there is no such thing as a contemplative life without the humility that takes us beyond the myth of our own grandeur to the cosmic grandeur of God. In the second, once we really know the grandeur of God we get the rest of life — ourselves included — in perspective. Reaching the moon told us how really insignificant we were in the universe. We begin to rethink all our dearly held notions of human consequence. Humility leads directly to contemplation.

Humility enables me to stand before the world in awe, to receive its gifts and to learn from its lessons. But to be humble is not to be diminished. Indeed, humility and humiliations are not the same thing. Humiliations degrade me as a human being. Humility is the ability to recognize my right place in the universe, both dust and glory, God's glory, indeed, but dust nevertheless.

The Rule of Benedict reminds the monastic to pray with the

psalmist, "I am a worm and not even human." What may sound to a me-centered generation like the destruction of human dignity is, in fact, its liberating truth. I am not, in other words, everything I could be. I am not even the fullness of myself, let alone a pinnacle for which my family, my friends, my world, the universe should strive. I am only me. I am weak often, struggling always, arrogant sometimes, hiding from myself most of the time, and always in some kind of need. I cover my limitations with flourish, of course, but down deep, where the soul is forced to confront itself, I know who I really am and what, on the other hand, however fine the image, I really am not. Then, the Rule of Benedict says, we are ready for union with God.

It is not when we become perfect — the whole idea of which becomes ever more suspect in a daily expanding universe — that we can claim God. It is when we accept the callow material that is ourselves that we can come to see beyond ourselves. It is when we cease to be our own god that God can break in.

The Rule of Benedict lays out the four dimensions of humility that lead to contemplation. The first calls us simply to recognize the presence of God in our lives. God, the Rule says quite clearly, simply is. God is with us whether we recognize that presence, that power, or not. God is not bought or gained or won or achieved. God is the ground of life. The point is not that we arrive at God; the point is that we cannot remove ourselves from God. We can only ignore the impact and the meaning of God's presence within us. "O God, come to my assistance," we say at the beginning of every prayer period of the day in my community. Even the desire to pray, we acknowledge, comes from the God within us.

The second level of humility requires us to accept the gifts of others, their Godself, their wisdom, their experience, even their direction. By revealing our inmost selves to someone else, we recognize the presence of God in others, yes, but we also free ourselves from the masks we wear and the lies which, in the end, are likely to fool even ourselves about us. For a woman it is the ability to realize that she is not nothing. For a man, it is the grace to understand that he is not everything. Open to the gifts of others and the truth of the self, we can see God where God is.

The third stage of humility requires us to let go of false expectations in daily life. When I am truly aware of my own littleness, I am not driven to spend life satisfying my ego more than my needs. I do not harbor the delusions of grandeur that compel a person to require the best car, the best chair, the best piece of meat on the plate, whatever the effect on others. The person full of God has much more security than any of the baubles of life — the comforts, the trappings, the titles, the symbols — can give.

The fourth level of humility reminds me to receive others kindly. Knowing my own limitations, I can accept theirs. Then I can walk through the world quietly, without bluster, without calling attention to myself and concentrated on the God within.

Finally, realistic about the self, the mind is free to become full of God.

To be a contemplative it is necessary every day to remember the God within. The posture is a crucial one. Only then can we empty ourselves of the need to play God that day, with anyone, in any way.

nteriority

Abba Isidore of Pelusia said: "Living without speaking is better than speaking without living. For a person who lives rightly helps us by silence, while one who talks too much annoys us. If, however, words and life go hand in hand, it is the perfection of all philosophy."

*I*T IS A HURRIED AND A NOISY WORLD in which we live. It is not an Egyptian desert of the third century. It is not a hermitage on a mountaintop. We are surrounded, most of us, at all times by the schedules and deadlines, the crowds and the distractions of a dense and demanding society.

We are an increasingly extroverted society, called away from our private selves on every level of life. Institutions even plan family events for us. They organize civic celebrations for us. They design financial plans for us. We spend the greater part of our lives meeting and satisfying the social requirements of institutions which, ironically, are supposedly designed to make personal expression possible and end up consuming us instead.

Even the spiritual responses people make to the God who created us are determined in large part by religious bodies that carry within themselves the traditions of the denomination from which they spring. But the contemplative knows that ritual and rite are not enough to nourish the divine life within. They are, at best, the appurtenances of religion. Spirituality is not the system we follow; it is the personal search for the divine within us all.

Interiority, the making of interior space for the cultivation of the God-life, is of the essence of contemplation. Interiority is the entering into the self to be with God. My interior life is a walk through darkness with the God within who leads us beyond and out of ourselves to become a vessel of divine life let loose upon the world.

Going into the self, finding the motives that drive us, the feelings that block us, the desires that divert us, and the poisons that infect our souls brings us to the clarity that is God. We find the layers of the self. We face the fear, the self-centeredness, the ambitions, the addictions that stand between us and commitment to the presence of God. We confront the parts of the self that are too tired, too disinterested, too distracted, to make the effort to nurture the spiritual life. We make space for reflection. We remind ourselves of what life is really all about. We tend to the substance of our souls.

No life can afford to be too busy to close the doors on chaos regularly: twenty minutes a day, two hours a week, a morning a month. Otherwise, we find in the middle of some long, lonely night when all of life seems unraveled and disoriented that somewhere along the line we lost sight of the self, became fodder in the social whirl and never even noticed until psychic darkness descended that it had happened to us.

The contemplative examines the self as well as God so that God can invade every part of life. We are an insulated society. We are surrounded by noise and awash in talk. We are smothered by a sense of powerlessness. And frustrated by it all, we suffer temper tantrums of the soul. The contemplative refuses to allow the noise that engulfs us to deafen us to our own smallness or blind us to our own glory.

Interiority is the practice of dialogue with the God who inhabits our hearts. It is also the practice of quiet waiting for the fullness of God to take up our emptiness. God lies in wait for us to seek the Life that gives meaning to all the little deaths that consume us day by day. Interiority brings us the awareness of the Life that sustains our life.

The cultivation of the interior life makes religion real. Contemplation is not about going to church, though going to church ought certainly to nourish the contemplative life. Contemplation is about finding the God within, about making sacred space in a heart saturated with advertisements and promotions and jealousies and ambitions, so that the God whose spirit we breathe can come fully to life in us.

To be a contemplative it is necessary to spend time every day stilling the raging inner voice that drowns out the voice of God in us. When the heart is free to give volume to the call of God that fills every minute of time, the chains snap and the soul is at home everywhere in the universe. Then the psyche comes to health and life comes to wholeness.

The fact is that God is not beyond us. God is within us and we must go inside ourselves to nourish the Breath that sustains our spirits.

ustice

Abba James said, "Just as a lamp lights up a dark room, so the fear of God, when it penetrates the heart, illuminates, teaching all the virtues and commandments of God."

*T*HERE IS A DANGER in the contemplative life. The danger is that contemplation is often used to justify distance from the great questions of life. Contemplation becomes an excuse to let the world go to rot. It is a sad use of the contemplative life and, at base, a bogus one. If contemplation is coming to see the world as God sees the world, then see it clearly we must. If contemplation means to become immersed in the mind of God, then we must come to think beyond our own small agendas. If contemplation is taking on the heart of God in the heart of the world, then the contemplative, perhaps more than any other, weeps over the obliteration of the will of God in the heart of the universe.

Contemplation, the search for the sacred in the tumult of time, is not for its own sake. To be a contemplative is not to spend life in a spiritual Jacuzzi, some kind of sacred spa designed to save humanity from the down and dirty parts of life. It is not an entree into spiritual escapism. Contemplation is immersion in the driving force of the universe, the effect of which is to fill us with the same force, the same care, the same mind, the same heart, the same will as that from which we draw. The mystics of every major religious tradition speak to what those concepts imply. "Within the lotus of the heart, God dwells," Hinduism tells us. "Buddha is omnipresent, in all places, in all beings, in all things, in all lands," the Buddhist master says. "Withersoever you turn, there is the Face of God; God is all embracing," Islam teaches. And Christianity reminds us always, "Ever since the creation of the world God's invisible nature, namely, God's eternal power and deity, has been clearly perceived in the things that have been made." But if all things are of God, then all things demand the soft hand of a caring God called justice.

Indeed, the teachings are traditional and the teachings are clear: God is not contained by any one people, in any single tradition. So must the contemplative respond to the divine in everyone. God wills the care of the poor as well as the reward of the rich. So, therefore, must the true contemplative. God wills the overthrow of the oppressor who stands with a heel on the neck of the weak. So does the real contemplative. God wills the liberation of human beings. So will the true contemplative. God desires the dignity and full human development of all human beings, and God takes the side of the defenseless. Thus must the genuine contemplative. Or, obviously, the contemplation is not real, cannot be real, will never be real because to contemplate the God of Justice is to be committed to justice.

True contemplatives, then, must do justice, must speak justice, must insist on justice. And they do. Thomas Merton spoke out against the Vietnam war. Catherine of Siena walked the streets of the city feeding the poor. Hildegard preached the word of justice to emperors and to popes. Charles de Foucauld lived among the poor and accepted the enemy. Benedict of Nursia sheltered strangers from the danger of the road and educated peasants. And so must we do whatever justice must be done in our time if we claim to be serious about sinking into the heart of God.

A spiritual path that does not lead to a living commitment to the bringing of the will of God is no path at all. It is a pious morass, a dead end on the way to God. Clearly, contemplation consigns us to a state of dangerous openness. It is a change in consciousness. We begin to see beyond boundaries, beyond denominations, beyond doctrines, dogmas, and institutional self-interest straight into the face of a mothering God from whom comes all the life that comes. To arrive at an awareness of the oneness of life and not to regard all of it as sacred trust is a violation of the very purpose of contemplation, the deepest identification of life with Life. To talk about the oneness of life and not to know oneness with all of life may be intellectualism, but it is not contemplation.

Contemplation is not ecstasy unlimited; it is enlightenment un-bounded by parochialisms, chauvinisms, genderisms, and class. The breath of God which the contemplative sets out to breathe is the breath of the spirit of compassion. The true contemplative weeps with those who weep and cries out for those who have no voice.

Transformed from within, the contemplative becomes a new kind of presence in the world, signaling another way of being, seeing with new eyes and speaking with new words the Word of God. The contemplative can never again be a complacent participant in an oppressive system. From contemplation comes not only the consciousness of the universal connectedness of life but the courage to model it as well.

The real contemplative takes the whole world in and shelters it, reveres it, and protects it with a body made of the steely substance of a justice that springs from love. To be contemplative it is necessary to reach out every day to the outcast other, just as does the God we breathe.

# Kindness

Once a brother committed a sin in Scetis, and the elders assembled and sent for Abba Moses. He, however, did not want to go. Then the priest sent a message to him, saying: "Come, everybody is waiting for you." So he finally got up to go. And he took a worn-out basket with holes, filled it with sand, and carried it along. The people who came to meet him said: "What is this?" Then the old man said: "My sins are running out behind me, yet I do not see them. And today I have come to judge the sins of someone else." When they heard this, they said nothing to the brother and pardoned him.

*T*HE DESERT MONASTICS ARE CLEAR: Self-righteousness is cruelty done in the name of justice. It is conceivable, of course, that we might find a self-righteous religious. It is feasible that we, like Abba Moses, could certainly find a self-righteous cleric. It is probable that I might very well find myself dealing with a self-righteous friend or neighbor or even family member. But it is not possible to find a self-righteous contemplative. Not a real contemplative.

Contemplation breaks us open to ourselves. The fruit of contemplation is self-knowledge, not self-justification. "The nearer we draw to God," Abba Mateos said, "the more we see ourselves as sinners." We see ourselves as we really are, and knowing ourselves we cannot condemn the other. We remember with a blush the public sin that made us mortal. We recognize with dismay the private sin that curls within us in fear of exposure. Then the whole world changes when we know ourselves. We gentle it. The fruit of self-knowledge is kindness. Broken ourselves, we bind tenderly the wounds of the other.

The most telling measure of the meaning of kindness in life is memories of unkindness in our own: scenes from a childhood marked by the cruelty of other children, recollections of disdain that scarred the heart, moments of scorn or rejection that leave a person feeling marginalized in the human community. In those moments of isolation we remember the impact of the fracturing of hope. We feel again the pain that comes with the assault on that sliver of dignity that refuses to die in us, however much the degradation of the moment. It is then that we come to understand that kindness, compassion, understanding, acceptance is the irrefutable mark of holiness because we ourselves have known — or perhaps have never known — the balm of kindness for which we so desperately thirsted in those situations. Kindness is an act of God that makes the dry dust of rejection digestible to the human psyche.

Cruelty is not the fruit of contemplation. Those who have touched the God who lives within themselves, with all their struggles, all their lack, see God everywhere and, most of all, in the helpless, fragile, pleading, frightened other. Contemplatives do not judge the heart of another by a scale on which they themselves could not be vindicated.

The pitfall of the religion of perfection is self-righteousness, that cancer of the soul that requires more of others than it demands of itself and so erodes its own fibre even more. It is an inner blindness that counts the sins of others but has no eye for itself. The self-righteous soul, the soul that preens on its own virtue, denies itself the self-knowledge that enables God to ignore what is lacking in us because our hearts are on the right way. It blocks the spirit of life from filling up the gaps within us that we ourselves are helpless to repair because the soul is not ready to receive.

Real contemplatives receive the other with the open arms of God because they have come to know that for all their emptiness God has received them.

To be a contemplative it is necessary to take in without reservation those whom the world casts out because it is they who show us most clearly the face of the waiting God.

Lectio
The Art of Holy Reading

One day some disciples came to see Abba Anthony. In the midst of them was Abba Joseph. Wanting to test them, the old man suggested a text from the scriptures and, beginning with the youngest, he asked them what it meant. Each one gave his opinion as he was able. But to each one of them the old man said, "You have not understood it." Last of all he said to Abba Joseph, "How would you explain this saying?" and Abba Joseph replied, "I do not know." Then Abba Anthony said, "Indeed, Abba Joseph has found the way, for he has said: 'I do not know.' "

CONTEMPLATION IS NOT A PRIVATE DEVOTION; it is a way of life. It changes the way we think. It shapes the way we live. It challenges the way we talk and where we go and what we do. We do not "contemplate" or "not contemplate." We live the contemplative life.

At the same time, there is one tool of the contemplative life which, in a special way, stirs the mind to new depths. It stretches the soul to new lengths. It expands the vision beyond all others. In the Rule of Benedict more time is allotted to this practice, for instance, than to any other activity except formal prayer. Thoughtful, reflective reading — *lectio* — immersion in the lessons of scripture and what the Rule of Benedict calls "other holy books," provides the background against which the entire rest of the life is lived. It is in *lectio* that the monastic mind comes to know itself.

The thoughtful reading of scripture does two things: it tells us what we bring to the Word of God, and it confronts us daily with what the word of God is bringing to us.

Monastic *lectio* is the practice of reading small passages daily — a page, a paragraph, a sentence — and then milking for meaning any word or phrase or situation that interests or provokes me there. Then the soul wrestling begins. The question becomes: Why does this word or passage mean something to me? Why is this word or situation bothering me? What does it mean to me, say to me? What feeling does it bring out in me? *Lectio* is a slow, reflective process that takes us down below the preoccupations of the moment, the distractions of the day to that place where the soul holds the residue of life.

Then the hard and wrenching part begins. Now, I must find in myself what this word, this sentence, this situation is asking of me. Here, in this place, at this time. Now. What is this awareness demanding of me and what is obstructing me from doing it? The answers come from everywhere: All the old memories bubble up, all the present struggles take on a new edge. Clearly, there is an emptiness in me that is in need of filling. There is a vision that needs forming. There is a courage of soul that needs honing. What is it?

Suddenly, perhaps, or painfully slowly, I begin to see into myself. The gulf opens up between what I am and what I must be if divine life is ever to come to fullness in me. There is no more concealing it from myself, no more ignoring it. There is nowhere to go now but into the heart of God with arms up and hands open. Then we open ourselves to the work of divinity in us, to the One who binds all brokenness together, to the Life that simmers in our deadest, driest parts.

Day after day, year after year, the contemplative goes down into the scriptures, back through the holy wisdom of the ages, out into the Truth of the time and, in each moment, learns something new about the struggle within, about divinity, about life. Contemplatives, like Abba Joseph, never really "know" what anything "means." They only come to know better and better in every sentence they read every day of their lives that divinity is at the depth of them calling them on.

To be a contemplative it is necessary to take time every day to fill myself with ideas that in the end lead my heart to the heart of the divine. Then, someday, somehow, the two hearts will beat in me as one.

Metanoia
Call to Conversion

One day Abba Arsenius was asking an old Egyptian man for advice. There was someone who saw this and said to him: "Abba Arsenius, why is a person like you, who has such a great knowledge of Greek and Latin, asking a peasant like this about your thoughts?" And Abba Arsenius replied, "Indeed, I have learned the knowledge of Latin and Greek, yet I have not learned even the alphabet of this peasant."

C HANGING THE WAY WE GO ABOUT LIFE is not all that difficult. We all do it all the time. We diet because we want to change the way we look. We learn to ski or fish or bowl or play pinochle when we want to change the patterns of our lives. We move to the country when we want to change the clatter of our environment. We change jobs, states, houses, relationships, lifestyles over and over again as the years go by. But those are, in the main, very superficial changes. Real change is far deeper than that. It is changing the way we look at life that is the stuff of conversion.

Metanoia, conversion, is an ancient concept that is deeply embedded in the monastic worldview. Early seekers went to the desert to escape the spiritual aridity of the cities, to concentrate on the things of God. "Flight from the world" — separation from the systems and vitiated values that drove the world around them — became the mark of the true contemplative. To be a contemplative in a world bent on materialism and suffocated with itself, conversion was fundamental. But conversion to what? To deserts? Hardly. The goal was purity of heart, single-mindedness of search, focus of life. Over the years, with the coming of the Rule of Benedict and the formation of monastic communities, the answer became even more clear. Conversion was not geographical. The flight was not from any one kind of location to another. We do not need to leave where we are in order to become contemplative. Otherwise, the Jesus who walked the dusty roads of Galilee surrounded by lepers and children and sick people and disciples and crowds of the curious and the committed was no contemplative either. Jesus the healer, the prophet, the preacher, the teacher, by that standard, was not engrafted into the mind of God. The thought appalls. No, surely contemplation is not a matter of place. "Flight from the world" is not about leaving any specific location. "Flight from the world" is about shedding one set of attitudes, one kind of consciousness for another. On the contrary, we simply have to be where we are with a different state of mind. We have to be in the office with the good of the whole world in mind. We have to be on the corporate board with the public at heart. We have to be in the home in a way that has more to do with development than with control. What Benedict wanted was conversion of heart.

But conversion to what?

The answer never changes. In every great religious tradition the concept is clear: To be contemplative we must become converted to the consciousness that makes us one with the universe, in tune with the cosmic voice of God. We must become aware of the sacred in every single element of life. We must bring beauty to birth in a poor and plastic world. We must restore the human community. We must grow in concert with the God who is within. We must be healers in a harsh society. We must become all those things that are the ground of contemplation, the fruits of contemplation, the end of contemplation.

The contemplative life is about becoming more contemplative all the time. It is about being in the world differently. What needs to be changed in us? Anything that makes us the sole center of ourselves. Anything that deludes us into thinking that we are not simply a work in progress, all of whose degrees, status, achievements, and power are no substitute for the wisdom that a world full of God everywhere, in everyone, has to teach us. Anything that drowns out the voice of the Ultimate within must be damped.

To become a contemplative, a daily schedule of religious events and practices is not enough. We must begin to do life, to be with people, to accept circumstances, to bring good to evil in ways that speak of the presence of God in every moment.

ature

A philosopher asked Saint Anthony: "Father, how can you be enthu-siastic when the comfort of books has been taken away from you?" And Anthony replied: "My book, O Philosopher, is the nature of cre-ated things, and whenever I want to read the word of God, it is right in front of me."

"WHERE IS GOD?" the catechism asked. "God is everywhere," the catechism answered. The answer is often ignored, but the answer, if God is really God, is certainly true. God is the stuff of the universe. In everything created resides the energy, the life, the image, the nature of the creator.

To know the creator, it is only necessary to study creation. The source of life is Life. The obvious is almost too simple to be believed: All life contains the secrets of Life. "In this acorn," the mystic Julian of Norwich said, "is everything there is." Nature, all of it, is the mirror of the Ultimate, the resting place of the God of life, the presence of the power of God.

Western religious tradition, unfortunately, in its intent to present God as a personal God, has inadvertently reduced God to a figure isolated and separate from creation, so other than ourselves that there is nothing of God in us. Our notion of God is God the great Engineer of the universe, who created spirit and matter, spun them into space, and left one to vie with the other. Spirit, this tradition

Illuminated Life

teaches, is the apotheosis of holiness; matter, on the other hand, is corruptible and corrupting. On the basis of this kind of thinking, nature is the illegitimate child of creation.

Nature, in a world that separates matter and spirit, exists only to be a kind of stage for human activity, a cornucopia of creature comforts, a wild world over which humanity was given "dominion" and through which God could finally be achieved only when matter was sloughed off. On such a strange scientific as well as spiritual foundation rests the justification for slavery, the rape of the earth, the wanton destruction of animals for "research," the validation for plundering the rain forests, burning holes in the ozone layer, and turning oceans into cesspools. But the contemplative knows a sin against nature is a sin against life.

It's a pitiable, and extremely limited, posture, this notion that matter is evil and spirit is good and the two are definitively separate. It reduces the Godhead itself to a thing, a creator separate from the creation that emanates from the very life energy that is God. It ignores the unlimited promise of life. It ignores the message of God who calls to us everywhere. It fails to understand that all of nature can exist without humanity but that humanity, with all its "dominion," cannot exist without the rest of nature. It ignores the oneness of life, the Oneness of God.

The contemplative knows better. The contemplative sees everywhere the One from whose life all life comes. All of life, the contemplative knows, reflects the face of God. To live with nature as an enemy is to fail life. To walk through nature as its dictator is to wrench the balance of life. To fail to see the voice of God in the balance of nature, the beauty of nature, the struggles of nature is to go through life blind of heart and deaf of soul.

To be a contemplative it is necessary to walk through nature softly, to be in tune with the rhythm of life, to learn from the cycles of time, to listen to the heartbeat of the universe, to love nature, to protect nature, and to discover in nature the presence and the power of God. To be a contemplative it is necessary to grow a plant, love an animal, walk in the rain, and profess our consciousness of God into a lifetime of pulsating seasons.

Illuminated Life

Openness

It was said about a disciple that he endured seventy weeks of fasting, eating only once a week. He asked God about certain words in the Holy Scripture, but God did not answer. Finally, he said to himself: "Look, I have put in this much effort, but I haven't made any progress. So I will go to see my brother and ask him."

When he had gone out, closed the door, and started off, an angel of God was sent to him and said: "Seventy weeks of fasting have not brought you near to God. But now that you are humble enough to go to your brother, I have been sent to you to reveal the meaning of the words." Then the angel explained the meaning which the old man was seeking, and went away.

*T*O CLOSE OURSELVES OFF from the wisdom of the world around us in the name of God is a kind of spiritual arrogance exceeded by little else in the human lexicon of errors. It makes of life a kind of prison where, in the name of holiness, thought is chained and vision is condemned. It makes us our own gods. It is a sorry excuse for spirituality.

The sin of religion is to pronounce every other religion empty and unknowing, deficient and unblessed. It is to ignore the call of God to us through the life and wisdom and spiritual vision of the other. The implications of that kind of closing out the multiple revelations of the mind of God are weighty: once we shut our hearts to the other, we have shut our hearts to God. It is a matter of great spiritual import, of deep spiritual summons. Openness to the presence of God, the Word of God in others, is of the essence of contemplation.

Learning to open the heart requires first that we open our lives. The home of whites that has never had a person of color at the

Illuminated Life

supper table is a home that has missed an opportunity to grow. People of color who have never trusted a white have missed a chance to confirm the humanity of the human race. The man who has never worked with a woman as a peer, better yet as an executive, has deprived himself of the revelation of the other half of the world. The comfortable contemplative who has never served soup at a soup kitchen, or eaten lunch in the kitchen with the cook, or clerked in a thrift shop, or spent time in inner-city programs lives in an insulated bubble. The world they know cannot possibly give them the answers they seek. The adult who has never asked a child a question about life and really listened to the answer is doomed to go through life out of touch and essentially unlearned. "When someone comes to the gate," the Rule of Benedict instructs, "say 'Benedicite.'" Say, in other words, "Thanks be to God" that someone has come to add to our awareness of the world, to show us another way to think and be and live beyond our own small slice of the universe.

Openness is the door through which wisdom travels and contemplation begins. It is the pinnacle from which we learn that the world is much bigger, much broader than ourselves, that there is truth out there that is different from our own. The voice of God within us is not the only voice of God.

Openness is not gentility in the social arena. It is not polite listening to people with whom we inherently disagree. It is not political or civil or "nice." It is not even simple hospitality. It is the munificent abandonment of the mind to new ideas, to new possibilities. Without an essential posture of openness, contemplation is not possible. God comes in every voice, behind every face, in every memory, deep in every struggle. To close off any of them is to close off the possibility of becoming new again ourselves.

To be a contemplative it is necessary to throw open the arms of our lives, to take in daily one experience, one person, one new idea with which we have no familiarity and ask what it is saying to us about us. Then God, the Ultimate Reality, the Life beyond life can come to us in deep, in rending, new ways.

 **rayer**

Abba Poemen said: "The nature of water is yielding, and that of a stone is hard. Yet if you hang a bottle filled with water above the stone so that the water drips drop by drop, it will wear a hole in the stone. In the same way the word of God is tender, and our heart is hard. So when people hear the word of God frequently, their hearts are opened to the fear of God."

*T*HERE IS ONLY ONE THING WRONG with the traditional defini-
tion of prayer: it misrepresents God. "Prayer," the old teaching
said, was "the raising of our hearts and minds to God." As if God
were some regal, distant judge outside ourselves. But science — with
its new perception that matter and spirit are of a piece, sometimes
particles, sometimes energy — suggests that God is not on a cloud
somewhere, imperious and suspecting. God is the very Energy that
animates us. God is not male humanity writ large. God is the Spirit
that leads us and drives us on. God is the voice within us calling us
to Life. God is the Reality trying to come to fullness within us, both
individually and together. It is to that cosmic God, that personal,
inner, enkindling God, that we pray.

Prayer is a long, slow process. First, it indicates to us how far we
really are from the mind of God. When the ideas are foreign to us,
when the process itself is boring or meaningless, when the quiet
sitting in the presence of God in the self is a waste of time, then

Illuminated Life

we have not yet begun to pray. But little by little, one gospel, one word, one moment of silence at a time, we come to know ourselves and the barriers we put between ourselves and the God who is trying to consume us.

The contemplative does not pray in order to coax satisfaction out of the universe. God is life, not a vending machine full of trifles to fit the whims of the human race. God is the end of life, the fulfillment of life, the essence of life, the coming of life. The contemplative prays in order to be open to what is, rather than to reshape the world to their own lesser designs.

The contemplative does not pray to appease a divine wrath or flatter a divine ego. The contemplative prays in order, eventually, to fall into the presence of God, to learn to live in the presence of God, to absorb the presence of God within. The contemplative prays until wordlessness takes over and presence is more palpable than words, more filling than ideas. One prayer at a time, the hard heart melts away, the satiated heart comes newly alive, the mind goes blank with enlightenment.

The contemplative is the one among us in whom prayer, deep reflection on the presence and activity of God in the self and the world, has come little by little to extinguish the illusions of autonomy and the enthronement of the self that make little kingdoms of us all. The contemplative goes beyond the self, and all its delusions, to Life itself. One prayer at a time, contemplatives allow the heart of God to beat in the heart they call their own.

The contemplative is the seeker who can go down into the self, down the tunnel of emptiness, and, finding nothing but God in the center of life, call that Everything. Most of all, the contemplative is the one who, looking at the world, sees nothing but the presence and activity of God everywhere, in everyone. How can this be possible? Because to be a contemplative, prayer is the key to the dialogue and, eventually, to the Silence that is Everything.

uest

Abba Poemen said to Abba Joseph: "Tell me how I can become a monastic." And Abba Joseph replied, "If you want to find rest here, and hereafter, say in every occasion, 'Who am I?'"

WHO IS THERE ANYWHERE in the world who is not looking for something: for approval, for money, for a home, for a career, for success, for security, for happiness? We are, by nature, spiritual foragers, seekers after grails. We look constantly for laurels and trophies cast in the crystal of time or the stardust of eternity. We are all on a quest for something. The distinguishing questions are two: For what am I seeking, and who am I as a result of the search?

Some people search for shadows on a wall and end in disillusionment. Others search for achievements cast in stone and, when the monuments to themselves crumble and fail to satisfy, end in discontent. Still more search from place to place at a frantic pace, tasting this, discarding that, demanding this, rejecting that till the very fury of the hunt exhausts their hearts and sears their souls. They are dabblers in life, connoisseurs of the superficial and the dissembling.

Illuminated Life

Who they are as a result of the search, other than earnest wanderers, even they do not know.

Religion — and spirituality — have their own kind of dilettantes, seekers who go from master to master, from system to system, from pious consolation to pious consolation, from spiritual posturings to spiritual escapes, but who never really appreciate the process, let alone the end of the journey. They seek but they never, ever find a home for the heart that lasts beyond the seeking. Religion — and spirituality — become bromides meant to ease a present pain or fill the current emptiness, rather than to take us below the urge of the seeking to find the source. We make religion our excuse for not finding God.

Indeed, there are people aplenty who use religion itself as a way to get the power they seek, the attention they crave, the comfort they need — and most of us are among them at one time or another. But they are not the contemplatives of the world.

Contemplatives do not take life as an obstacle to insight, going from taste to taste until the taste buds of the soul go dry. Contemplatives do not wander from church to church, from guru to guru trying to find a formula outside of themselves to fill up what is missing inside themselves. Contemplatives do not need to go anywhere at all to find where God waits to meet them on the road of the self. The contemplative simply stands in place and in the standing answers the question "Who am I" with the answer "I am the one who waits for the God within." I am, in other words, the one who pursues the center of life. I am the one who goes behind every system to the source. I am the one who is in search of the Light that is distant from my darkened soul and alien to my restless mind and extraneous to my scattered heart. I am the one who realizes that the distance between God and me is me.

To lead a contemplative life requires that we watch what we're seeking—and why we're seeking it. Even good can become noise in the heart when we do it, not because it's right, but because it will in turn do something for us: Bring us status. Make us feel good. Give us security. Require little of our own lives.

God is more consuming, more fulfilling than all those things. The grail we seek is God alone. But talking about God is not the same as searching for God, all the simple saints, all the fallen hierarchs to the point. To be a contemplative we must seek God in the right places: within the sanctuary of the centered self.

e-creation

Once two brothers went to visit an old monastic. It was not the old man's habit to eat every day. When he saw the brothers, however, he welcomed them with joy and said: "Fasting has its own reward, but if you eat for the sake of love you satisfy two commandments, for you give up your own will and also fulfill the commandment to refresh others."

*I*T'S NOT SOMETHING that most of us like to admit, but the truth is that "fasting," any disciplinary or dour approach to life — relentless concentration on work, duty, responsibilities, business, productivity — has its own rewards. However difficult the work itself may seem to those who watch us do it, there is something secretly very satisfying about the ardor of doing it. Giving up Spartan routines to visit old relatives or play with children, to write personal mail or take the dog for a walk, to go fishing or have a picnic supper on the shore makes the hardy and virtuous cringe at the very thought of it. We are serious people, too absorbed by important things for those things. We are too "busy" to be human.

So, we drone on through life, wearing our sensitivities to a frazzle. We go from day to day drowning our mind in more of the same instead of letting it run free in new fields of thought or new kinds of experience or new moments of beauty. We just keep doing the same things over and over again. Worst of all, we consider ourselves spiritually noble for doing them. Virtue becomes the blinders of our soul. We never see the God who is everywhere because we never look anyplace but where we've looked before.

Re-creation, holy leisure, is the mainstay of the contemplative soul, and the theology of Sabbath is its cornerstone. "On the seventh day," scripture says, "God rested." With that single image, that one line of Holy Writ, reflection, re-creation of the creative spirit, transcendence, the right to be bigger than what we do, is sanctified. To refuse to rest, to play, to run loose for awhile on the assumptions that work is holier, worthier of God, more useful to humankind than refreshment, strikes at the very root of contemplation.

Life is about more than work. Work is useless, even destructive, if its purpose goes awry. What will keep work pristine if not the contemplative eye for truth and the contemplative compass for everything God called good? Recreation is the act of stretching the soul. When we stop the race to nowhere, when we get off the carousel of productivity long enough to finally recognize that it is going in a circle, we reclaim a piece of our own humanity.

The purpose of recreation is to create a Sabbath of the soul. We need time to evaluate what we have done in the past. Like God, we must ask if what we spend our lives doing is really "good" for anyone. For me? For the people who will come after me? For the world in which I live right now?

We must assess the impact of our daily work on the lives of those around us. We must ask ourselves whether what we are doing with our lives and the way we are doing it is really worth the expenditure of a life, either our own or the lives of those with whom we come in contact. Only Sabbath, only re-creation gives me the chance to step back and think, to open up and be made new, to walk through life with eyes up and heart open, to expand the human parts of my human experience.

Life is not meant to be dismal. Life is not an endurance test. Life is life, if we make it that. How do we know for sure that life is meant to be an excursion into joy? Because there is simply too much to enjoy: fishing water in a back bay, the view from a mountaintop, wild berries on the hill, a street dance in the neighborhood, a good book, the parish bazaar, the city culture, the family reunion.

Religious traditions that refuse to enjoy life, reject life. But religion that rejects life is no religion at all. It fails to connect the sacred now with the sacred beyond. To be a contemplative we must bring ourselves to life so that all of life can mediate God to us.

**ilence**

One of the elders said, "Just as it is impossible to see your face in troubled water, so also the soul, unless it is clear of alien thoughts, is not able to pray to God in contemplation."

*S*ILENCE IS THE LOST ART in a society made of noise. Radios wake us up, and timers on TVs turn off the day-full of programs long after we have gone to sleep at night. We have music in cars and elevators and office waiting rooms. We have surround-sound that follows us from the living room to the kitchen to the upstairs bath. We have public address hookups in every office building and large, loud, screaming sound systems mounted on street corners. We exercise with earphones on and tape recorders strapped to our belts. We lie on beaches with our ears cabled to portable CD players. We surround ourselves and immerse ourselves in clatter. Racket and jingle, masking as music and news and sitcoms, have become the sound barriers of the soul in this society. They protect us from listening to ourselves.

What the contemplative knows that modern society has forgotten, it seems, is that the real material of spiritual development is not in books. It is in the subject matter of the self. It is in the things we

Illuminated Life

think about, in the messages we give ourselves constantly, in the civil war of the human soul that we wage daily. But until we are quiet and listen, we can never, ever know what is really going on — even in ourselves. Especially in ourselves.

Silence frightens us because it is silence that brings us face to face with ourselves. Silence is a very perilous part of life. It tells us what we're obsessing about. It reminds us of what we have not resolved within ourselves. It shows to us the underside of ourselves, from which there is no escape, which no amount of cosmetics can hide, that no amount of money or titles or power can possibly cure. Silence leaves us with only ourselves for company.

Silence is, in other words, life's greatest teacher. It shows us what we have yet to become, and how much we lack to become it. "Wherever I am," the poet Mark Strand writes, "I am what's missing."

Silence, the contemplative knows, is that place just before the voice of God. It is the void in which God and I meet in the center of my soul. It is the cave through which the soul must travel, clearing out the dissonance of life as we go, so that the God who is waiting there for us to notice can fill us.

A day without silence is a day without the presence of the self. The pressure and pull of a noisy day denies us the comfort of God. It is a day in which we are buffeted by the world around us and left at the mercy of the clatter and jangle of our own hearts. To be a contemplative we must put down the cacophony of the world around us and go inside ourselves to wait for the God who is a whisper, not a storm. Silence not only gives us the God who is Stillness but, just as importantly, teaches the public self of us what to speak.

Time

A brother came to see Abba Theodore and started to talk and inquire about things which he himself had not tried yet. The old man said to him: "You have not found a boat or put your gear into it, and you haven't even sailed, but you seem to have arrived in the city already. Well, do your work first; then you will come to the point you are talking about now."

ONE OF THE OBSESSIVE CONCERNS of contemporary society is speed. Everything we produce we produce to go faster than the ones before it. Planes go faster than the speed of sound, though no one cares. Cars are sold for their capacity to go from zero to sixty miles an hour in seconds, as if anyone ever needed to. Computer upgrades costing hundreds of dollars are downloaded every day to take milliseconds off the operating speeds of the versions before them. To be valuable now, everything must go faster, start up more quickly, work at speeds measured in numbers no mind can calculate. We want instant oatmeal, electronic ticketing, accelerated educational programs, weekend college courses, and world news in thirty seconds or less. We are "a people on the move." We want results. We are not a people who believe in process anymore, much as we love to talk about it.

But the spiritual life, the desert monastics knew, does not operate in high gear at high speed. The spiritual life — contemplation — is a slow, slow uncovering of the mechanics of the soul and the even slower process of putting it all back together again, of coming to see what we never saw before — God everywhere and, most of all, in us.

Ironically enough, in our haste, our generation has lost a sense of the value of time. Speed has not saved us time. It has simply enabled us to fill it with twice as much work as we used to do. The faster we go, the more we leave ourselves behind. We do not stop for sunsets anymore. We take pictures of them, instead, and then never take time to look at the pictures again.

But there are some things that cannot be hurried. We cannot hurry the process of grief, for instance. We cannot rush the project of growth. We cannot speed the effects of hurt. We cannot hasten the coming of love. We must not attempt to flit through the search for God and then, failing in the enterprise of a lifetime, call it fruitless. Each of those things comes in stages. Each of them takes soul-work.

Time, the contemplative knows, is given not for the sake of perfection but for the sake of discovery. There is a great deal to be discovered in life before we are finally able to break ourselves open to the God within and around us out of whom all life flows. What we learn in the course of a lifetime, the contemplative comes to realize, is life-changing:

We must learn that no institution is God. Nothing that symbolizes God is God and cannot be absolutized.

We must learn that we are not God. The world was not made for our amusement; it was made for our growth. And grow we must, painful as the growing may be.

We must learn that the God who is not contained in any institution and who is the very breath we breathe, is in us waiting for us to come to that realization. We must stop looking for God in things. God is here.

Finally, we must learn that time is the gift of realization, not the death of all our dreams. Whatever is happening, whatever stage in which we find ourselves, is the stuff of God. And the more we have of it, the more we have of God in the now.

To be a contemplative we must begin to see time, not as a commodity, but as a sacrament revealing God to us in the here and now. Always.

nderstanding

Some disciples came to see Abba Poemen and said to him: "Tell us, when we see brothers dozing during the sacred office, should we pinch them so they will stay awake?" And the old man said to them: "Actually, if I saw a brother sleeping, I would put his head on my knees and let him rest."

*U*NDERSTANDING — COMPASSION — is the foundation of a monastic lifestyle. Without it there is no hope at all for developing a community out of strangers. The Rule of Benedict is brimming with the concept: Monastics are not to bother the procurator of the monastery at undue times. People are not here simply to meet our demands. The doorkeeper is to welcome guests kindly at any hour, day or night. When people have needs we must do what we can to meet them. Monastics who need more than the rule allots are to be given it, no questions asked. The person is always more important than the rule. Meal servers are to be fed before the others so their work is no harder than necessary. No one exists for our satisfaction. Monastics who fail to live the life as they promised they would are to be counseled as well as corrected. All faults are forgivable; all life is a succession of stages. It is a Rule, in other words, that knows the limitations of the human condition—and honors them.

Life is not perfect and people are not perfectible. Only understanding, only compassion — the ability to bear life with the rest of humanity, whatever burdens the bearing brings — perfects us. When that concept gets lost in the name of religion, gets forgotten in the name of goodness, religion has gone awry and virtue has lost its meaning. God is compassionate and gives us what we need. No one can possibly be truly contemplative, truly in touch with the God-life, truly infused by the spirit of God, who does anything less for the sake of the other.

Contemplation is the mirror through which we come to touch the greatness of God, yes, but contemplation is also the filter through which we discern the scope of our smallness and the potential of our greatness at the same time. The contemplative looks for perfection nowhere but in God. The contemplative understands brokenness. And, most of all, the contemplative realizes that it is precisely at the point of personal need that God comes to fill up the emptiness that is us.

The contemplative knows that what we lack is our clear claim we have to the fullness of God. Not to know what we lack is to become our own gods, a more than sickly substitute for the real thing. When contemplation, that absorption in God that fills a person with the consciousness of the presence of God everywhere, in everyone, is real, we are consumed with love. There is no one for whom we do not care, no one who is beneath us. God, we know, is where we least of all expect God to be, waiting for us to realize that.

Then, when we come to realize all of that, it becomes perfectly plain: There is no rule that means more than the person in front of us. There is no sin too great to be forgiven. There is no need that must not be reckoned with. There is no suffering I can rightly ignore. There is no struggle I can condemn. There is no pain I am not obliged to bear.

God understands. And so, therefore, does the real contemplative.

ision

Abba Zacharias had a vision. He told his spiritual Father, Carion the ascetic, about it. Exasperated, Carion beat him and told him the vision came from demons. Zacharias went to Abba Poemen to tell him about it. Seeing his sincerity, Abba Poemen sent him on to a monk who was a mystic. This monk knew all about the vision before Zacharias even told him and said it was indeed from God. Then the mystic instructed him, "Now go back and submit yourself to your father."

*T*HE DESERT MONASTICS ARE VERY CLEAR: Vision is one thing; visions are another. Visions are psychological phenomena that, in the end, may have nothing whatsoever to do with the way a person lives life or how a person develops. Some visions are surely spiritual gifts, but many of them are just as surely products of heightened emotional systems. Some of the most contemplative figures in history, for instance, never had a "vision." Hildegard did not. Meister Eckhart did not. Teresa of Avila did not. They knew the presence of God, but they never claimed to have had a single physical demonstration of it. Instead of visions, they had vision.

Vision is not physical. It is a quality of the soul. People with vision hone in, laser-like, to the presence of God in life. They see the holy, bleeding, suffering, feuding world as God sees the world: as one and as sacred. In love with a loving God, they are impelled to love God's world as God does. They set out to love it as God loves it. They see God everywhere and in everything. They stretch beyond

Illuminated Life

the demands of the personal, the chauvinistic, the nationalistic, the sectarian, even the doctrinal, to the will of God for the entire world. They are not trapped by the pitiful little agendas of color or gender or hierarchy or place. They live possessed by the will of God for the world and spend themselves for its coming. They do not slide into spiritual complacency or affect spiritual elitism. They work at the spiritual life, expecting no gifts from it and seeking no mystical signs to mark their spiritual growth. They simply do what must be done: They immerse themselves in the presence of God until everything becomes for them the presence of God.

Contemplation is not the stuff of charlatans, telepathists, and magicians. Contemplation is about very basic, very real things. It is about seeing God in everyone, finding God everywhere, and responding to all of life as a message from God. Contemplation is not a road show of visions. It is not spiritual snake oil. It is not an exalted state of being. It is simply consciousness of the Ultimate in the immediate.

Genuine spirituality is not spent escaping from life to live in a mental state of unconcern or otherworldliness. Contemplatives do not seek "visions." They simply seek to know God, the God present in them and around them, in others and in everything, in Goodness and Truth, in universal love and universal peace. To contemplatives God is not a magic trick. God is the very breath they breathe.

To be contemplatives, we must have the vision to do every day whatever must be done to make God present in this place, at this time, whatever the cost.

ORK

One of the elders said: "I never wanted work which was useful to me but a loss to others. For I have this expectation, that what helps the other is fruitful for me."

And Abba Theodore of Pherme said, "In these days many take their rest before God gives it to them."

I N THIS SOCIETY, work has become the way we make money, the way we enable ourselves to do what we would really prefer to do if we didn't need to work. No other approach to life, perhaps, explains so clearly what has really happened to the quality of the world around us than this. If there is anything that measures spiritual depth in a work-oriented society, it is surely the work we do, and why we do it or, conversely, the work we won't do and why we won't do it.

Work is the contemplative's response to contemplative insight. In fact, it is everybody's answer to the profundity — or the shallowness — of their ideas about creation. To know the presence of God in all things has serious implications for the way a person lives the rest of life. What we know determines what we do. When I float in a sea of God, there is nothing not sacred. "Treat all things" — the buckets and the plants and the spades and the land — "as vessels of the

Illuminated Life

altar," the Rule of Benedict instructs. It is a profoundly contemplative statement.

In the sacredness of the universe the contemplative sees the face of God. To do anything that defiles that face in the name of anything unworthy of the God who created it — profit, greed, leisure, progress, industry, "defense" — is blasphemy.

One of the most demanding, but often overlooked, dimensions of the creation story is that when creation was finished, it wasn't really finished at all. Instead, God committed the rest of the process to us. What humans do on this earth either continues creation or obstructs it. It all depends on the way we look at life, the way we see our role in the ongoing creation of the world.

Work is our contribution to creation. It relates us to the rest of the world. It fulfills our responsibility to the future. God left us a world intact, a world with enough for everyone. The contemplative question of the time is what kind of world we are leaving to those who come after us. The contemplative sets out to shape the world in the image of God. Order, cleanliness, care of the environment bring the Glory of God into the stuff of the moment, the character of the little piece of the planet for which we are responsible.

The ideal state, the contemplative knows, is not to avoid work. The first thing Genesis requires of Adam and Eve is that they "till the garden and keep it." They are, then, commanded to work long before they sin. Work is not, in Judaeo-Christian tradition, punishment for sin. Work is the mark of the conscientiously human. We do not live to outgrow work. We live to work well, to work with purpose, to work with honesty and quality and artistry. The floors the contemplative mops have never been better mopped. The potatoes the contemplative grows do not damage the soil they grow in under the pretense of developing it. The machines a contemplative designs and builds are not created to destroy life but to make it more possible for everyone. The people the contemplative serves get all the care that God has given us.

The contemplative is overcome by the notion of "tilling the garden and keeping it." Work does not distract us from God. It brings the reign of God closer than it was before we came. Work doesn't take us away from God. It continues the work of God through us. Work is the priesthood of the human race. It turns the ordinary into the grandeur of God.

To be a real contemplative and no shaman of the airy-fairy, I must work as if the preservation of the world depends on what I am doing in this small, otherwise insignificant space I call my life.

Xenophilia
The Love of Strangers

Amma Sarah said: "If I pray to God that all people might be inspired because of me, I would find myself repentant at the door of every house. I would rather pray that my heart be pure toward them than that I changed something in theirs."

*I*T IS NOT WHAT OTHERS THINK OF US; it is what we think of others that singles the contemplative out in a crowd. Our role in life is not to convert others. It's not even to influence them. It certainly is not to impress them. Our goal in life is to convert ourselves from the pernicious agenda that is the self to an awareness of God's goodness present in the other. It is no idle prayer. The beauty of the open soul is not easy to come by in a world where the other — the alien, the foreigner, the stranger — threatens my sense of security and the pyramids of social control. After all, we know who's meant to be in charge, and we cannot allow outsiders to jeopardize a system built on the absolutes we have devised for ourselves.

We learn at a very early age in this culture that the world is at our disposal. Most clearly of all, we learn that we are its norm. We know we are its pinnacle. We suffocate from national chauvinism. The messages are only insinuated, of course, but clear nevertheless: Other cultures are not nearly so "modern" or "progressive" or "developed" — meaning civilized — as we are. Other ethnic groups are not nearly so clever, so polished. Other races not nearly so human. There is a hierarchy of human achievement and, history shows, economics dictate, power insists, we are it.

"We" and "they" are the hallmarks of an age awash in refugees, under siege from immigrants, and yet inseparably linked in a world in which there are no more natural boundaries. We have, indeed, one world now, but though intricately intertwined, painfully stratified. It is a world, a city, a neighborhood full of many of their kind and some of our kind. We, it is clear, have a natural right to everything we need to live in dignity and security. They are required to wait for such things or work harder to get them or, sometimes, to stand by and watch while we use up what they lack. In the midst of it all, in order to defend some of us from the rest of them, the world ends up dealing with struggles for jobs, conflict over food stamps, wars for water, wars for land, and, saddest of all, wars for ethnic cleansing.

But the social problem is one thing. The spiritual problem is another. The reality is that those struggles, those wars are not else-where. Those wars take place in the human heart. We have become a world of insiders and outsiders when, in reality, there is no such thing as an outsider anymore. The whole city, the whole world lives in our living rooms. The whole city, the whole world is warring for my heart. Only the contemplative lives well in a world the security of which depends on the open heart.

There are few things in life more threatening to the person whose religion is parochialism than the alien and few things more revelatory to the contemplative than the stranger. The contemplative sees in the other what is lacking in the self. It is in the stranger that God's new word comes most clearly to light for those who behold behind appearances the refraction of the divine mystery in a mundane world.

The stranger, to the contemplative, is the angel of Tobias, the visitor to the tent of Abraham and Sarah, the sound of "Hail, Mary" in the garden calling us to a life we do not know and cannot predict. It is the stranger who disarms all our preconceptions about life and penetrates all our stereotypes about the world. It is the stranger who makes the supernatural natural. It is the stranger who tests all our good intentions.

To be a contemplative we must open our hearts and our doors to the stranger in whom lives the Word that is calling to our boundaried hearts to become wider than denominationalism alone can ever make us. To be a contemplative we must live in peace. We must speak peace everywhere to everyone. We must speak good about everyone we do not know and yet do know to be just as full of God as we are, if not more so.

 **earning**

Abba Nilus said: "Do not want things to turn out as they seem best to you but as God pleases. Then you will be free of confusion and thankful in your prayer."

W HO IS THERE who hasn't, at some time or other, wanted life to be different than it is? Who of us has not wanted it ourselves? We get tired of what we're doing or where we are. We look for better days somewhere else. We want to do something different but, down deep, we don't really know what it is. All we know is that we yearn for what we do not have. We feel the confusion. We lack the gratitude for life of which the desert monastics speak. We chafe and groan through life. And so we miss it. Life ends and we have not lived it. We yearn for the more we cannot see.

Contemplation is also yearning. But the contemplative knows that no matter where we go — and go we must if the call is clear — we will still, in the end, be yearning for what cannot be seen. Yearning is, in fact, a sign of the spiritual life. Those who do not yearn for God do not know God. But yearning for God requires that we allow the Life within us that is the energy of the universe to connect us to Life everywhere, in every one, at all times, always.

Contemplation is the magnet of the soul. It draws us out of ourselves and more deeply into ourselves at the same time. It is always restless, always at peace. What is here is everything and what is here is never enough. The contemplative yearns always for the Light that suffuses all of life but is yet only a glimmer here of the total Mystery in which we are immersed.

Contemplation is the giving over of the self to oneness with the One who is the life of the entire universe, the One of which everything is part, but nothing is all. It is joy and pain at the crossroads. It is Awareness writ large and daily life full to the brim. It is God everywhere and nowhere. The implications astound us: To be contemplative means to live in the presence of God and the absence of God at the same time.

The life of the contemplative is spent nurturing the presence of the Ultimate and hungering after the absence of the Ultimate always. To the contemplative, Life is only the beginning of awareness. Death is only the birth canal to new life, the process by which we are expelled out of the womb of the world into the womb of God, out of life lived in darkness into Life lived in light.

The contemplative enjoys — and the contemplative yearns. Life is everything and life is empty. Life is meant to be lived to the full.

The only question for the restless soul is: For what do we yearn? If we yearn only for more of ourselves, we will never be satisfied because in our smallness we are not enough for ourselves. If we yearn for God, we will not be satisfied either but we will at least know that we have what we are alive to discover: the Glory of God in me.

To be a contemplative it is necessary to say every day what the ancients of every tradition have been telling us over and over again for eons, "God is in me and I am of God and so I and everything are one. Alleluia."

 **eal**

Abba Lot went to see Abba Joseph and said to him, "Abba Joseph, as far as I am able I say my little office, I keep my little fasts, I pray my little prayers, I meditate a little, I live in peace, and as far as I can, I purify my thoughts. What else can I do?" Then Abba Joseph, stood up and stretched his hands toward heaven. His fingers became like ten torches of flame and he said to him, "Why not be turned completely into fire?"

"WHO CAN SEE GOD AND LIVE?" the ancients asked. It's an important question. While we look for marks of our spiritual progress, the measure may well be in the question: Who can see God and live the same dull, directionless, complacent way they lived before God became the presence in life that makes all other presence relative? God is not in the whirlwind, the prophet Ezekiel says. Indeed not, the contemplative knows. Rather, God is the whirlwind. God is the energy that drives us, the torch that leads us, the life that beckons us, the Spirit within that carries us on — past every doubt, beyond every failure, despite every difficulty. To that Energy there is no acceptable, no possible, response but energy. Those who have no flame in their hearts for justice, no unrelenting understanding of the other, no consciousness of responsibility for the reign of God, no awareness of a prodding, nagging call to stretch themselves beyond themselves, no raging commitment to human community, no vision of beauty, and no endurance for the dailiness of it all may

Illuminated Life

indeed be seeking God, but make no mistake, God is still only an idea to them — precious as it may be — but not a Reality.

Contemplation is a very dangerous activity. It brings us not only face to face with God. It brings us, as well, face to face with the world, face to face with the self. And then, of course, something must be done. The presence of God is a demanding thing. Nothing stays the same once we have found the God within. We become new people and, in the doing, see everything around us newly, too. We become connected to everything, to everyone. We carry the world in our hearts: the oppression of peoples, the suffering of friends, the burdens of enemies, the raping of the earth, the hunger of the starving, the dreams of every laughing child. Awareness focuses our hearts. Zeal consumes us.

Zeal, "the burning point" in Greek, has to do with caring enough about something to have made being born worthwhile. Without it, life is, at best, time spent between a useless beginning and a futile end. To live without believing in something enough to spend a life for it is dull existence.

Zeal can go awry, of course. Zeal not grounded in God is a plague of the spirit. It becomes anti-Semitism, capital punishment, witch burnings, homophobia, sexism, nuclear war. Zeal grounded in a small God becomes the Inquisition, the Taliban, excommunications, shunnings, and canonical silencings. "There is a good zeal that leads to life," the Rule of Benedict teaches, "and a harsh and evil zeal that leads to death." The warning is clear: we can put ourselves in the place of God rather than in the arms of God. To be driven by anything less than the God of Love and so ourselves to love less recklessly everything, everyone on earth, is to risk evil zeal in the name of the God of vengeance.

To be contemplative we must have zeal for the God of Love in whom all things have their beginning and their end. We must be turned completely into fire. Fortunately, we will know when that happens because we will find ourselves consumed with love not only for God but for everything, everyone God created. There is no clearer sign of contemplation. Then, and only then, is our own zeal safe to unleash upon the world.

Across the Centuries

Abba Anthony said: "The time is coming when people will be insane, and when they see someone who is not insane, they will attack that person saying: 'You are insane because you are not like us.'"

W E SO OFTEN THINK that those who refuse under any conditions to deny the essential goodness of life are mad. Look at the suffering. Look at the evil. Be real, we say. We are so often inclined to think that those who continue to see life where life seems to be empty and futile are, at best, foolish. Be sensible, we say. But in that case, we may be the ones who are mad. The truth is that contemplation, the ability to see behind the obvious to the soul of life, is the ultimate sanity. The contemplative sees life as it really is under all the struggle and the pain: imbued with God, glowing with eternity, full of energy, and so overflowing with good that evil never totally triumphs.

Contemplation keeps the inner eye focused on Goodness. But contemplation is as important for what it is not as for what it is. Contemplation is not a spiritual fad or some kind of religious trick. It does not come as a fringe benefit of extreme asceticism, nor is it the automatic by-product of mesmerizing rituals. It is not mental imbalance posing as religion. Contemplation is the crown of the spirit, the gateway of the heart through which all good comes and in which all things are welcome as gifts of God. Contemplation exists across time, across traditions, beyond cultures, outside of creeds, despite denominational cautions or priestly prescriptions to the contrary. Awareness of the presence of God in the stuff of the daily, the everywhere, the always, the everyone, undergirds every major spiritual path. The faithful only believe in God. Seekers see God everywhere. Seekers see what others cannot even imagine: the presence of God in the things of the daily. The critical difference between those who are godly and those who are contemplative is that, having come to see God in the world in which they are immersed, contemplatives never cease to see again, however unbelievable the circumstances may be. It is not the contemplative who is mad. It is the rest of the world who lack what it takes to be sane in an often insane world.

The desert monastics put it this way: As he was dying Abba Benjamin taught the disciples his last lesson. "Do this," he said, "and you will be saved: Rejoice always, pray constantly, and in all circumstances give thanks."

In the end, the fruit of contemplation is joy. When we walk with God, what is there to fear? Serenity comes to those who walk with God. Surety comes to those who see God in everything. Peace comes to those who know that what is, is of God, if we will only make it so.

Most of all, joy, praise, and gratitude live in the hearts of those who live in God. It is not the joy of fools. The contemplative knows evil when it rears its head. It is not the praise of the ingratiating. The contemplative knows struggle when difficulties come. It is not the gratitude of the obtuse. The contemplative recognizes the difference between chaff and grain. The contemplative knows that grain is for bread, but the contemplative also knows that chaff is for heat. The contemplative realizes that everything in life has for its purpose the kindling of the God-life within us. And so the contemplative goes on with joy and resounds with praise and lives in gratitude. Always. What better way to bring the light of the diamond to glow in darkness.

Bibliography

Citations of the desert monastics are from the following:

Nomura, Yushi. *Desert Wisdom: Sayings from the Desert Fathers*. Garden City, N.Y.: Image Books, 1984.

The Sayings of the Desert Fathers: The Alphabetical Collection. Trans. Benedicta Ward. Kalamazoo, Mich.: Cistercian Publications, 1975.

Others sources cited are as follows:

Hillesum, Etty. *An Interrupted Life*. New York: Pantheon Books, 1983.

Jäger, Willigis. *Search for the Meaning of Life: Essays and Reflections on the Mystical Experience*. Ligouri, Mo.: Triumph Books, 1995.

Wilson, Andrew, ed. *World Scripture: A Comparative Anthology of Sacred Texts*. New York: Paragon House, 1991.

Joan Chittister, OSB
is the Executive Director of

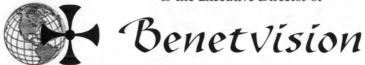

Benetvision

research and resources
for contemporary spirituality

"a point of view with the future in mind"

For a complete catalogue
of our materials contact us at:

Benetvision
355 East Ninth Street
Erie, PA 16503-1107

phone: 814-459-5994
fax: 814-459-8066
e-mail: msbpr@juno.com

See the Benetvision section of
the Benedictine Sisters of Erie web page:

www.erie.net/~erie-osb